The Barcelona Game

Stephen Rabley

Level 1

Series Editors: Andy Hopkins and Jocelyn Potter

1.1 What's the book about?

Look at the front of this book and talk about these questions.

1 Where is Barcelona? What do you know about it? What can visitors do there?

2 Why are the people in this story going to visit Barcelona? What do you think?

3 What games do you like? Do you like playing them or watching them? Why?

1.2 What happens first?

1 **Read page 1 of *The Barcelona Game* quickly and answer these questions.**

    1 Where do the Hoopers live?

      a London   **b** Cardiff   **c** (Manchester)

    2 How old is Holly?

      a 11   **b** 12   **c** 13

    3 How many brothers has she got?

      a 2   **b** 3   **c** 4

    4 When are Manchester United playing in Spain?

      a On Tuesday   **b** On Wednesday   **c** On Thursday

    5 Who is going to Spain with Kev and Trev?

      a Their mum   **b** Their dad   **c** Holly

    6 What is Holly doing on page 1?

      a She is reading.   **b** She is shouting.   **c** She is dancing.

    7 Does Holly like football?

      a Yes   **b** No   **c** Perhaps

2 **Which of these people are going to go to Spain? What do you think?**

Holly Hooper lives in Manchester. She has two brothers, Kev and Trev. Holly is twelve, quiet and loves books. The boys are seventeen, noisy and love football.

One September morning, Kev runs into the kitchen.

'They're here!' he **shout**s. 'The tickets for the Barcelona game are here!'

He dances across the kitchen floor.

Holly is reading *Oliver Twist*. She puts her book down.

'The Barcelona game?' she asks. 'What's that?'

Trev looks at her. 'You don't know?' he says. 'Manchester United are playing in Spain on Wednesday. **Dad**, Kev and I are going.'

'Oh,' Holly says.

shout /ʃaʊt/ (v) Please don't *shout*. I can hear you!
dad /dæd/ (n) I go home from school with *Dad* because he is a teacher here.

1

But that evening
Dad isn't well. **Next** morning
he talks to Kev and Trev.

'I'm sorry, boys,' he says. 'I've
got a bad cold. I can't go to . . .
to . . . ACHOO! . . . to Spain
with you.'

'But, Dad, we've got three tickets
for the aeroplane,' Kev says. 'And three
tickets for the game.'

'And a hotel room for you too,' Trev says. 'What are we going to do?'

The room is quiet.

Then **Mum** says, 'I know! You can take Holly.'

Kev looks at Trev. Trev looks at Kev.

'Yes!' Dad says. 'That's the answer. It *is* the summer holidays. And
she's doing Spanish at school too.'

'But . . . ' Kev and Trev say.

'No "buts",' Mum says.
'You're taking your little
sister with you!'

next /nekst/ (adj) Is Manchester the *next* stop on this train?
mum /mʌm/ (n) *Mum* works in an office. She comes home at six o'clock.

The next day is Wednesday.
Kev, Trev and Holly **leave** for
Spain. Holly is very happy.
On the aeroplane she reads a
book about Barcelona. There
are a lot of photos in it.

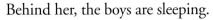

'It's a beautiful place,'
she thinks.

Behind her, the boys are sleeping.

They arrive at Barcelona airport at three o'clock.

'OK,' Trev says. 'Let's take a taxi to the hotel.'

Then Holly says, 'Oh, no!' and stops suddenly. She can see a big
hole in her bag. Some of her books are falling on the floor.

Kev looks at Trev. Trev looks at Kev.

'This is a good start,' Kev says.

Then he sees a small airport shop. There are some bags in the
window. They have *Barcelona* on them.

'Go and buy a new bag,' he **tell**s Holly. 'But be quick, OK?'

leave /liːv/ (v) The train *leaves* Beijing in the evening and arrives in Moscow five days later.
hole /həʊl/ (n) There is a *hole* in your shirt. Did you know?
tell /tel/ (v) The children are in bed. Please *tell* them a story.

3

Holly buys one of the Barcelona bags. Then she and her brothers take a taxi to their hotel. Holly goes into her room. It has two windows and a very big bed.

'This is **great**,' she thinks.

Then she goes into Kev and Trev's room.

'OK, what are we going to do before the game?' she asks. 'We can see the **cathedral** or the famous street, "Las Ramblas", or the Olympic **Stadium** or . . . '

'No, no, no,' Kev says. 'We don't want to go to those places. We're going to Tibidabo. It's a **funfair**. Trev's friend went there in April. It's great, he says.'

'A funfair!' Holly says. 'But . . . '

'No "buts",' Kev says. 'I'm telling you, it's great. We're going there – and you're coming with us.'

great /greɪt/ (adj) We are going to stay in a *great* hotel. Do you want to come with us?
cathedral /kəˈθiːdrəl/ (n) The big building near the river is St Paul's *Cathedral*.
stadium /ˈsteɪdiəm/ (n) We are going to a football game in the new *stadium*.
funfair /ˈfʌnfeə/ (n) We had a very good day at the *funfair*, but now we haven't got any money.

4

Later, Holly and the boys arrive at Tibidabo.

'Look – there's a big **wheel**!' Trev says. 'I love big wheels.'

'Me too,' Kev says. 'Let's go!'

Holly looks at the wheel. 'Oh no,' she thinks.

Five minutes later, the wheel stops.

'That was great,' Trev says. 'Let's do it again.'

Then he looks at Holly. Her face is white.

'Are you all right?' he asks.

'No,' Holly says. 'I'm not.'

Kev looks at Trev. Trev looks at Kev.

'OK – listen,' Kev says. 'You see that café? Go and wait for us there. But stay there and *don't move*, OK?'

'OK,' Holly says.

'And put the tickets in your bag,' Kev says. 'We don't want to take them with us. See you at seven o'clock, OK?'

'Yes, Kev,' Holly says.

She puts the tickets in her bag. Then she walks to the café.

wheel /wiːl/ (n) The London Eye is a big *wheel*. You can see a lot of buildings from the top because it moves slowly.

2.1 Were you right?

**Look at the answers to Activities 1.1 and 1.2 on page ii. Were you right?
Then finish these sentences with words from the box.**

bag	friend	Spanish	café	book	wheel	cold	taxi

1 Dad doesn't go to Spain because he has got a ....cold............... .

2 Holly's doing .... at school.

3 On the aeroplane she reads a .... about Barcelona.

4 At Barcelona airport she buys a new ....

5 Holly, Kev and Trev take a .... to their hotel.

6 Trev's .... went to Tibidabo in April.

7 Holly doesn't like the big .... at the funfair.

8 Holly waits for Kev and Trev in a ....

2.2 What more did you learn?

Who is talking? Write the letters, A–E.

1 'I can't go to – ACHOO! – Spain with you.' ◯

2 'You can take Holly.' ◯

3 'OK, what are we going to do before the game?' ◯

4 'Are you all right?' ◯

5 'And put the tickets in your bag.' ◯

2.3 Language in use

Look at the sentences in the box. Then look at the pictures and finish sentences 1–6.

> She's **doing** Spanish at school.
>
> You're **coming** with us.

1 Holly / read / book .... *Holly is reading a book.* ....

2 Kev and Trev / sleep / aeroplane ....

3 Holly / buy / new bag ....

4 Why / you / look / me? ....

5 Holly's books / fall / floor ....

6 Kev / talk / sister ....

2.4 What happens next?

1 Which is the right word?

a At the café, Holly is *happy / unhappy.*

b She *does / doesn't* like funfairs.

c The tickets are in her *hotel room / bag.*

d She wants to see Las Ramblas, a famous *cathedral / street.*

e Kev and Trev are going to see her in the café at *6 o'clock / 7 o'clock.*

2 What do you think? Write *Yes* or *No*.

a Is Holly going to stay in the café? ....

b Is she going to have a problem with the tickets? ....

c Is she going to see Las Ramblas? ....

7

At the café *La Masia*, Holly sits down. She asks for coffee. Then she looks at her Barcelona book.

'I wanted to see these places,' she thinks. 'And now I'm not going to see them. I'm in Spain and I'm only going to see a game of football.'

Her coffee comes and she drinks it. Ten minutes later, a man sits at the next table. He has a **moustache** and a brown coat. He has a bag with *Barcelona* on it. Holly sees the bag and smiles.

'He's got one too,' she thinks. Then she looks at her book again.

moustache /mə'stɑːʃ/ (n) His hair is black, but he has a long white *moustache*.

The man drinks two black coffees, and after that he leaves. Holly closes her book on Barcelona.

'Now what?' she thinks. 'It's only six o'clock.'

Suddenly she remembers *Oliver Twist* and smiles.

Her bag is on the floor. Holly opens it, but then she stops smiling. A blue shirt? An American newspaper? An address book with the name 'Fred Burns' on it?

'These aren't my things,' she thinks. 'I don't understand. Where's my book? Where are the tickets for the . . . ?'

Then she closes her eyes. 'Oh no. The man with the moustache. This isn't my bag. It's *his*!'

She stands up. Suddenly her hands are cold. Where is he? *Where is he*? She runs out of the café. There are a lot of people in the street. Holly looks left and right.

'I can't see him,' she thinks.

A boy on a **motorbike** is **pass**ing the café. He sees Holly's face and stops.

'What's wrong?' he asks her.

She starts to tell him. Then she looks across the street. A taxi is driving away. Fred Burns is sitting in the back.

'That's him!' she shouts. 'There he goes. He's got my bag. Stop! *Stop*!!!'

motorbike /ˈməʊtəbaɪk/ (n) He went across Europe on the back of his brother's *motorbike*.
pass /pɑːs/ (v) We *are passing* the shops, but we can't stop. We haven't got time.

'He can't hear you,' says the boy. 'The **traffic**'s very noisy. Listen – do you want to **follow** him?'

Holly looks at the boy. 'How? On your motorbike?'

'Yes.'

Holly thinks about it. 'OK,' she says.

The boy gives her a **crash helmet**. 'Put this on,' he says.

Holly sits behind him and puts it on.

'What's your name?' she asks.

'Pere,' the boy answers.

Then he starts the bike and drives quickly away.

Holly closes her eyes. Fred Burns's taxi is yellow and black. It goes left, right and left again very quickly. Pere follows it. Holly opens her eyes. They are passing a big building. She remembers one of the photos in her book.

'That's the Olympic Stadium,' she thinks.

traffic /ˈtræfɪk/ (n) There is a lot of *traffic* in this street because people drive their children to the school.
follow /ˈfɒləʊ/ (v) I know the place. *Follow* me!
crash helmet /ˈkræʃ ˌhelmɪt/ (n) People can't see your face under that *crash helmet*.

Ten **minute**s later, Fred Burns's taxi is in the famous street, Las Ramblas. Holly can see her bag in the back window. She can see Fred Burns too.

'Please stop!' she thinks. 'Where are you going?'

There are some traffic lights in front of them. They go from green to yellow. The taxi passes the lights, but then the lights go red. Two old women start to walk across the street. They have got a lot of **flower**s in their hands.

'Oh no,' Holly says. She looks at the back of Fred Burns's head. 'We can't catch him now.'

'Yes, we can,' Pere shouts.

He drives in front of the two women very quickly. One says, '*Aiieee*!!'

'Sorry!' Pere shouts and drives away.

---

minute /'mɪnɪt/ (n) Work starts in ten *minutes*. We are going to be late.
flower /'flaʊə/ (n) His mother is ill. He is taking her some *flowers*.

12

Pere follows the taxi for a long time. Then it stops near Barcelona's famous cathedral. Holly and Pere stop too. There are a lot of people and cars in front of the cathedral.

'It's a beautiful building,' Holly thinks.

Then she remembers Fred Burns.

'Look – there he is,' Pere says. 'He's getting out of the taxi.'

Holly takes off her crash helmet.

'Stop!' she shouts. 'Mr Burns! Please stop.'

She gets off the bike and starts to run.

3.1 Were you right?

Look at your answers to Activity 2.4. Were you right? Now answer these questions. Write *Holly, Fred* or *Pere*.

1   Who has a moustache?   ....

2   Who says, 'He's got my bag!'?   ....

3   Who gives Holly a crash helmet?   ....

4   Who is American?   ....

5   Who has a brown coat?   ....

6   Who sits behind Pere on his motorbike?   ....

7   Who drives in front of two women on Las Ramblas?   ....

3.2 What more did you learn?

Put these sentences in the right order. Write 1–8 in the boxes.

a   A boy on a motorbike is passing the café.

b   Holly and Pere pass the Olympic Stadium.

c   A man sits next to Holly at the Café La Masia.

d   'Sorry!' Pere shouts and drives away.

e   Fred Burns gets out of his taxi at Barcelona cathedral.

f   Holly finds an address book with the name 'Fred Burns' on it.

g   Two old women start to walk across Las Ramblas.

h   Holly gets onto the boy's motorbike.

3.3 **Language in use**

Look at the words in the box. Then finish the paragraph with these words.

> She looks **across** the street.
>
> Fred Burns is sitting **in** the back.

after	in front of	next to	near	at	off
	across	out of	in	on	with

Holly is sitting .... Fred Burns .... Café La
Masia. He leaves .... her bag and she runs ....
the café. Pere is passing .... a motorbike. He stops and looks
.... Holly. 'What's wrong?' he asks. They follow Fred Burns's
taxi, but there are some traffic lights .... them. Two old
women walk .... the street, but Pere drives very quickly. After
a long time, Fred Burns's taxi stops .... the cathedral. Then
Pere stops his motorbike too, and Holly runs .... Fred Burns.

3.4 **What happens next?**

It is 6.35. Holly, Pere and Fred Burns are at the cathedral. Kev and Trev
are at Tibidabo. Who is talking in these pictures? Write the name of the
person and the letter of the right picture.

1 'Run! He's going into the
  cathedral!'
  .....Pere........ ......E.....

2 'Excuse me. You've got my bag.'
  ....

3 'What time is it, Trev?'
  ....

4 'Who are you, and how do you
  know my name?'
  ....

5 'This is a great funfair, Kev.'
  ....

15

Pere watches the English girl. She is running very quickly. Fred
Burns is walking into the cathedral. The American hears his name
and stops.

'Me?' he says.

He looks left and right. Then he sees Holly. She runs to him and
starts talking. Two minutes later, she comes back to Pere. There is a
big smile on her face.

'Have you got the right bag now?' he asks.

'Yes, I have.' Holly is very happy. 'Oh, Pere, thank you. How can
I . . . ?' But then she stops smiling. 'Oh, no.
What time is it?'

Pere looks at his watch.
'Twenty to seven. Why?'

Suddenly Holly's face
is white again.

'Kev and Trev. They're
going to be at *La Masia*
in twenty minutes.'

She tells Pere about her brothers and the football game.

'I understand,' the Spanish boy says. 'OK – put your helmet on again.'

Pere and Holly drive back to *La Masia* very quickly. They pass a lot of beautiful old buildings.

'This is great,' Holly thinks. 'I'm seeing Barcelona now.'

Five minutes later, she and Pere pass the big wheel at Tibidabo.

'What time is it now?' Holly asks.

'One minute to seven,' the Spanish boy says. 'It's OK. You're not going to be late.'

He stops in front of the café. Holly looks at the people there.

'Good,' she says. 'Kev and Trev aren't here.'

Then she gets off the motorbike.

'Pere – how can I thank you?' she says.

'That's OK,' Pere answers. 'I had a good time.'

He looks at his motorbike. There are two red flowers in one of the wheels.

'Here,' he says, and he gives the flowers to Holly. 'These flowers are for you. Have a good time at the game, OK?'

He smiles and starts his bike. Then he drives away.

Kev and Trev arrive at the café. Holly is reading *Oliver Twist*. She looks up.

'Oh, hello,' she says. 'Are we going now?'

There are a lot of people in the Nou Camp football stadium. Kev, Trev and Holly get there ten minutes before the game.

'Have you got the tickets?' Kev asks his sister.

'Yes,' Holly says, and she takes them from her bag.

The boys buy food and drinks. Then they all sit down.

'We had a great time this afternoon,' Trev says.

'Yes,' Kev says. 'A great time.'

'Good,' Holly says. 'Me too.'

Kev looks at Trev. Trev looks at Kev. Then they look at their little sister and smile.

'You!' Kev says. 'Holly, you *never* have . . .'

But the players are coming into the stadium.

'United! United!' Kev and Trev shout.

Holly looks at them.

'Yes, *me*,' she thinks. '*I* had a great time.'

She smiles. Then she opens *Oliver Twist* and starts to read.

Look at the picture. Holly and Pere are talking. What are they saying? Work with a friend.

| Student A | You are Pere. Ask Holly about her visit to Barcelona and her home in England. |
| Student B | You are Holly. Answer Pere's questions. Then ask him questions. |

Write about it

Holly is writing about Barcelona. Put these words in the right places.

visit	Olympic	street	Spain	football	funfair	beautiful

Barcelona is in .... It has a very
.... cathedral, a big .... stadium
– the Nou Camp – and an .... stadium too.
Las Ramblas is a famous .... in Barcelona. And
there's Tibidabo, a big .... A lot of people
.... Barcelona every year.

QUESTIONS, QUESTIONS, QUESTIONS

1 **After the summer holidays, Holly's friends ask a lot of questions about her visit to Barcelona. What do they ask about:**

- Barcelona?
- Pere?
- her family?
- the football game?
- Fred Burns?

Start your questions with these words:

How many ...?	What ...?	Which ...?	Where ...?
Who ...?	Why ...?	When ...?	Do ...?	Did ...?
Is ...?	Are ...?	Was ...?	Were ...?	

1 ....

2 ....

3 ....

4 ....

5 ....

6 ....

7 ....

8 ....

9 ....

10 ....

ANSWERS, ANSWERS, ANSWERS

2 **Work with a friend. Ask and answer the questions in Activity 1.**

My brothers wanted to see the football game.

Why did you go to Barcelona?

3 Now write an article for a school newspaper about Holly's visit to Barcelona.

Holly Hooper's
visit to
Barcelona

Barcelona

'An American man walked out with my bag.'

Holly Hooper went to Spain in the summer holidays.

'I'm doing Spanish at school.'

'Barcelona is a very beautiful place.'

'I don't like football.'

Nou Camp Stadium

22